GREAT QUOTES FROM GREAT WOMEN

GREAT QUOTES FROM GREAT WOMEN

COMPILED BY PEGGY ANDERSON • ILLUSTRATED BY MICHAEL MCKEE

CELEBRATING EXCELLENCE PUBLISHING

We are grateful to Encyclopedia Britannica, Inc.
for permission to reprint its copyrighted materials
and use their 1991, 15th edition as the primary source
for biographical information.

GREAT QUOTES FROM GREAT WOMEN compiled by Peggy Anderson

Illustrations by Michael McKee

ISBN: 1-880461-26-9

4 5 6 7 8 Printing/AK/Year 97 96 95 94 93

Table Of Contents

*Dedicated with love
and gratitude to my mother
Mary Crisorio and my mentor
Ann Gilchrist.*

$\mathcal{P}$reface

Great Women are not considered so because of personal achievements but for the effect their efforts have had on the lives of countless others. From daring feats of bravery to the understated ways of a compassionate heart, great women possess a common strength of character. Through their passion and persistence, they have advanced womanhood and the world.

The insights herein come from major female influencers of the arts, entertainment, science, politics, religion, law, medicine, social causes and sports. Some figures are well-known; others are the unfamiliar names of unsung heroes. While each deserves our deepest consideration, the selected group of profiles features pioneers in their fields, crusaders for humanity and catalysts of change.

These are timeless examples of individuals unafraid to challenge the status quo. These are lives and words worth remembering.

Peggy Anderson

*E*leanor Roosevelt was a United Nations diplomat, humanitarian and wife of President Franklin D. Roosevelt.

During her twelve years as First Lady (1933 - 1945), the unprecedented breadth of her activities and advocacy of liberal causes made her nearly as controversial a figure as her husband. Roosevelt instituted regular White House press conferences for women correspondents for the first time. In deference to the President's illness, she helped serve as his "eyes and ears" throughout the nation, embarking on extensive tours around the country. She showed particular interest in such humanitarian concerns as child welfare, slum clearance projects and equal rights.

After President Roosevelt's death (1945), President Harry Truman appointed her a delegate to the United Nations, where, as chairman of the UN Commission on Human Rights, she played a major role in the drafting and adoption of the Universal Declaration of Human Rights.

Eleanor Roosevelt was one of the most widely admired women in the world and remains an inspiration to many.

ELEANOR ROOSEVELT
1884 - 1962

*"It is better to light a candle than
to curse the darkness."*

*"Remember no one can make you feel
inferior without your consent."*

*"It is not fair to ask of others what you
are not willing to do yourself."*

*"The future belongs to those who believe
in the beauty of their dreams."*

ELEANOR ROOSEVELT
1884 - 1962

"I listen and give input only if somebody asks."

Barbara Bush
1925
First Lady of the United States
and Humanitarian

"Light tomorrow with today."

Elizabeth Barrett Browning
1806 - 1861
English Poet

"It is easy to be independent when you've got money. But to be independent when you haven't got a thing— that's the Lord's test."

Mahalia Jackson
1911 - 1972
American Gospel Singer

"One is not born a woman, one becomes one."

Simone De Beauvoir
1908 - 1986
Philosopher and French Writer

"Mistakes are part of the dues one pays for a full life."

Sophia Loren
1934
Italian Actress

"The only thing that makes one place more attractive to me than another is the quantity of heart I find in it."

Jane Welsh Carlyle
1801 - 1866
Scottish Poet

"But men never violate the laws of God without suffering the consequences, sooner or later."

Lydia M. Child
1802 - 1880
American Abolitionist, Writer and Editor

"Beauty is in the eye of the beholder."

Margaret Wolfe Hungerford
1855 - 1897
Irish Writer

Susan B. Anthony is best remembered as a pioneer and crusader of the women's suffrage movement in the United States. President of the International American Suffrage Association, her work helped pave the way for the Nineteenth Amendment to the Constitution, giving women the right to vote.

Discouraged by the limited role women were allowed in the established temperance movement, Anthony helped form the Woman's State Temperance Society in New York, one of the first organizations of its kind.

She devoted herself with vigorous determination to the anti-slavery movement, serving from 1856 to the outbreak of the war in 1861, when she worked as an agent for the American Anti-Slavery Society.

Organizing the International Council of Women in 1888 and the National Woman Suffrage Alliance in 1904, Susan B. Anthony was a major catalyst for social change in America and abroad.

SUSAN B. ANTHONY
1820 - 1906

"Men their rights and nothing more; women their rights and nothing less."

~ ❧ ~

"...Gentlemen...Do you not see that so long as society says a woman is incompetent to be a lawyer, minister or doctor, but has ample ability to be a teacher, that every man of you who chooses this profession tacitly acknowledges that he has no more brains than a woman?"

~ ❧ ~

"...The day will come when men will recognize woman as his peer, not only at the fireside, but in councils of the nation. Then, and not until then, will there be the perfect comradeship, the ideal union between the sexes that shall result in the highest development of the race."

~ ❧ ~

"Failure is impossible."

SUSAN B. ANTHONY
1820 - 1906

"*Love is not enough. It must be the foundation, the cornerstone—but not the complete structure. It is much too pliable, too yielding.*"

Bette Davis
1908 - 1991
American Actress

"*Think wrongly, if you please, but in all cases think for yourself.*"

Doris Lessing
1919
British Writer

"*Creative minds have always been known to survive any kind of bad training.*"

Anna Freud
1895 - 1982
Austrian Psychotherapist
and daughter of Sigmund Freud

"*The beauty of the world, which is so soon to perish, has two edges, one of laughter, one of anguish, cutting the heart asunder.*"

Virginia Woolf
1882 - 1941
British Writer

"Enemies are so stimulating."

Katharine Hepburn
1909
American Actress

"How strange when an illusion dies, it's as though you've lost a child."

Judy Garland
1922 - 1969
American Singer and Actress

"The future is made of the same stuff as the present."

Simone Weil
1909 - 1943
French Revolutionary, Theologian and Philosopher

"Look twice before you leap."

Charlotte Brontë
1816 - 1855
English Writer

*H*elen Adams Keller was born in Tuscumbia,
Alabama in 1880. A severe illness in infancy left her deprived
of sight, hearing, and the ability to speak. Her life represents
one of the most extraordinary examples of a person who was
able to transcend her physical handicaps.

Through the constant and patient instruction of Anne Sullivan,
Helen Keller not only learned to read, write and speak, but
went on to graduate cum laude from Radcliffe College in 1904.
In addition to becoming the author of several articles, books
and biographies, she was active on the staffs of the American
Foundation for the Blind and the American Foundation for the
Overseas Blind. She also lectured in over twenty-five countries
and received several awards of great distinction.

Helen Keller's courage, faith and optimism in the face of such
overwhelming disabilities had a profound effect on all she
touched. Her tremendous accomplishments stand as a symbol
of human potential.

HELEN KELLER
1880 - 1968

"Keep your face to the sunshine and you cannot see the shadows."

"I thank God for my handicaps, for through them, I have found myself, my work, and my God."

"Security is mostly a superstition. It does not exist in nature, nor do the children of men as a whole experience it. Avoiding danger is no safer in the long run than outright exposure. Life is either a daring adventure or nothing."

"It gives me a deep, comforting sense that things seen are temporal and things unseen are eternal."

HELEN KELLER
1880 - 1968

"An archaeologist is the best husband a woman can have. The older she gets the more interested he is in her."

Agatha Christie
1891 - 1975
English Writer

"There were angry men confronting me and I caught the flashing of defiant eyes, but above me and within me, there was a spirit stronger than them all."

Antoinette L. Brown
1825 - 1921
The First Woman in the United States
to be ordained as a Minister

"Love from one being to another can only be that two solitudes come nearer, recognize and protect and comfort each other."

Han Suyin
1917
Chinese Writer and Physician

"You can't give people pride, but you can provide the kind of understanding that makes people look to their inner strengths and find their own sense of pride."

Charleszetta Waddles
1912
American Nun and Writer

"We've chosen the path to equality, don't let them turn us around."

Geraldine A. Ferraro
1935
The First Woman nominated as
Vice-President of the United States

"The brain is not, and cannot be, the sole or complete organ of thought and feeling."

Antoinette Brown Blackwell
1825 - 1921
American Feminist and Writer

"I've had an exciting life; I married for love and got a little money along with it."

Rose Kennedy
1890
Mother of President John F. Kennedy

"When so rich a harvest is before us, why do we not gather it? All is in our hands if we will but use it."

Elizabeth Seton
1774 - 1821
The First American Saint

*M*argaret Thatcher was the first woman in European history to be elected prime minister.

The daughter of a grocer, she received her degree in chemistry at Oxford, where she became president of the University Conservative Association. During the 1950's, she worked as a research chemist and also studied law, specializing in taxation.

Thatcher ran for Parliament in 1950, but it was not until 1959 that she was finally elected to the House of Commons. She served as parliamentary secretary to the Ministry of Pensions and National Insurance, and later as secretary of state for education and science. She was elected the leader of the Conservative Party in 1975, and the party's victory in the 1979 elections elevated her to the office of prime minister.

Margaret Thatcher became known as the Iron Lady because of her dedication to the ideals in which she believed and the grace to get them accomplished.

MARGARET THATCHER
1925

"*You may have to fight a battle more than once to win it.*"

❧

"*What is success? I think it is a mixture of having a flair for the thing that you are doing; knowing that it is not enough, that you have got to have hard work and a certain sense of purpose.*"

❧

"*Let our children grow tall and some taller than others if they have it in them to do so.*"

❧

"*To wear your heart on your sleeve isn't a very good plan; you should wear it inside, where it functions best.*"

MARGARET THATCHER
1925

"*Yes, I have doubted. I have wandered off the path, but I always return. It is intuitive, an intrinsic, built-in sense of direction. I seem always to find my way home. My faith has wavered but saved me.*"

Helen Hayes
1900 - 1993
American Actress and Writer

"*Diets, like clothes, should be tailored to you.*"

Joan Rivers
1933
American Comedienne and Television Talk Show Host

"*I've never sought success in order to get fame and money; it's the talent and the passion that count in success.*"

Ingrid Bergman
1915 - 1982
Swedish Actress and Playwright

"*I tell myself that God gave my children many gifts—spirit, beauty, intelligence, the capacity to make friends and to inspire respect...There was only one gift he held back—length of life.*"

Rose Kennedy
1890
Mother of President John F. Kennedy

"I wasn't afraid to fail. Something good always comes out of failure."

Anne Baxter
1923
American Actress

"I am not a has-been. I'm a will be."

Lauren Bacall
1924
American Actress

"Many a humble soul will be amazed to find that the seed it sowed in weakness, in the dust of daily life, has blossomed into immortal flowers under the eye of the Lord."

Harriet Beecher Stowe
1811 - 1896
American Writer

"If you have made mistakes, even serious ones, there is always another chance for you. What we call failure is not the falling down, but the staying down."

Mary Pickford
1893 - 1979
American Actress

*M*other Teresa, born Agnes Gonxha Bojarhiu,
is revered for her lifelong dedication to the poor,
most notably the destitute masses of India.

In 1928, at the age of eighteen, she went to Ireland to join
the Institute of Blessed Virgin Mary, and shortly thereafter
traveled to India to work with the poor of Calcutta. After
studying nursing, she moved into the slums of the city and
founded the Order of the Missionaries of Charity. Mother
Teresa was summoned to Rome in 1968 to found a home for
the needy, and three years later she was awarded the first
Pope John XXIII Peace Prize. By the late 1970's,
the Missionaries of Charity numbered more than
1,000 nuns who operated 60 centers in Calcutta and
over 200 centers worldwide.

Mother Teresa's selfless commitment to helping the poor
saved the lives of nearly 8,000 people in Calcutta alone. Her
compassion and devotion to the destitute earned her the
Nobel Peace Prize in 1979.

MOTHER TERESA
1910

"We can do no great things—
only small things with great love."

"I am a little pencil in the hand
of a writing God who is sending a
love letter to the world."

"I do not pray for success. I ask
for faithfulness."

"Loneliness and the feeling of being
unwanted is the most terrible poverty."

MOTHER TERESA
1910

"Where large sums of money are concerned, it is advisable to trust nobody."

Agatha Christie
1891 - 1975
English Writer

"We fought hard. We gave it our best. We did what was right and we made a difference."

Geraldine A. Ferraro
1935
The First Woman nominated as
Vice-President of the United States

"Only you and I can help the sun rise each coming morning. If we don't, it may drench itself out in sorrow."

Joan Baez
1941
American Folksinger and Civil Rights Activist

"Nothing in science has any value to society if it is not communicated."

Anne Roe
1904
American Psychologist and Writer

"Our whole way of life today is dedicated to the removal of risk. Cradle to grave we are supported, insulated, and isolated from the risks of life— and if we fall, our government stands ready with Bandaids of every size."

Shirley Temple Black
1928
American Diplomat and Actress

"I have learned from experience that the greater part of our happiness or misery depends on our dispositions and not on our circumstances."

Martha Washington
1732 - 1802
Former First Lady of the United States

"The artist has always been and still is a being somewhat apart from the rest of humanity."

Beatrice Hinkle
1874 - 1953
American Psychiatrist and Writer

"When you get into a tight place and it seems you can't go on, hold on, for that's just the place and the time that the tide will turn."

Harriet Beecher Stowe
1811 - 1896
American Writer

$\mathscr{P}$olish-born French physicist, Marie Curie was
famous for her work on radioactivity. From childhood, she
was remarkable for her prodigious memory and intellect.

One of Curie's outstanding achievements was to have
understood the need to accumulate intense radioactive
sources, not only for the treatment of illness, but also to
maintain an abundant supply for research in nuclear
physics. Her insights paved the way for other researchers
to discover the neutron and artificial radioactivity.
Shortly after this discovery, however, Marie Curie
died from leukemia caused by the action of radiation.

Twice a winner of the Nobel Prize, Marie Curie
made immense contributions to physics because of
her influence on subsequent generations of nuclear
physicists and chemists.

MARIE CURIE
1867 - 1934

"*One never notices what has been done;
one can only see what remains
to be done.*"

~ ❧ ~

"*Nothing in life is to be feared.
It is only to be understood.*"

~ ❧ ~

"*You cannot hope to build a better
world without improving the individuals.
To that end each of us must work
for his own improvement, and at the
same time share a general responsibility
for all humanity, our particular duty
being to aid those to whom we think
we can be most useful.*"

~ ❧ ~

"*I was taught that the way of progress
is neither swift nor easy.*"

MARIE CURIE
1867 - 1934

"I don't need a man to rectify my existence. The most profound relationship we'll ever have is the one with ourselves."

Shirley MacLaine
1934
American Actress and Writer

"The soul can split the sky in two, and let the face of God shine through."

Edna St. Vincent Millay
1892 - 1950
American Poet and Writer

"Painting's not important. The important thing is keeping busy."

Grandma Moses
1860 - 1961
American Artist

"The devotion of thought to an honest achievement makes the achievement possible."

Mary Baker Eddy
1821 - 1910
Founder of the Christian Science Religion

"The more visible signs of protest are gone, but I think there is a realization that the tactics of the late sixties are not sufficient to meet the challenges of the seventies."

Coretta Scott King
1927
American Lecturer, Writer,
and Civil Rights Activist

"Reality is something you rise above."

Liza Minnelli
1946
American Actress and Singer

"All talk of women's rights is moonshine. Women have every right. They have only to exercise them."

Victoria Claffin Woodhull
1838 - 1927
First Woman nominated to the Presidency of
the United States

"If I had one wish for my children, it would be that each of them would reach for goals that have meaning for them as individuals."

Lillian Carter
1898 - 1984
Mother of President Jimmy Carter

*B*orn a slave in Maryland, Harriet Tubman
yearned to be free. In 1849, she made her escape to
Pennsylvania through the Underground Railroad. She then
used that route nineteen more times, returning to the South
to lead more than 300 slaves to freedom.

As the years passed, Tubman became known as the "Moses"
of her people, directing them out of enslavened land.
During the Civil War, she served the Union Army as a
nurse and a spy. With black soldiers she mobilized an effort
to free slaves who had not been released by their masters.

Following the war, Tubman raised funds to construct
schools for ex-slaves. She labored for female suffrage and, in
1903, established a shelter for poor, homeless blacks.

An American heroine, Harriet Tubman is remembered as
an extraordinary humanitarian.

HARRIET TUBMAN
1820 - 1913

"*I* had reasoned this out in my mind,
there was two things I had a right to,
liberty and death. If I could not have one,
I would have the other, for no man
should take me alive."

"*I* had crossed the line, I was free; but
there was no one to welcome me to the
land of the freedom. I was a stranger in
a strange land."

"*When* I found I had crossed that line,
I looked at my hands to see if I was the
same person. There was such a glory over
every thing; the sun came like gold
through the trees, and over the fields, and
I felt like I was in Heaven."

"*I* should fight for my liberty as long
as my strength lasted, and when the
time came for me to go, the Lord would
let them take me."

HARRIET TUBMAN
1820 - 1913

"Habits do not like to be abandoned, and besides they have the virtue of being tools."

Charlotte Painter
1926
American Writer

"I realized that if what we call human nature can be changed, then absolutely anything is possible. From that moment, my life changed."

Shirley MacLaine
1934
American Actress and Writer

"If I didn't believe the answer could be found, I wouldn't be working on it."

Dr. Florence Sabin
1871 - 1953
First Female Professor at a Medical School

"The trouble is, if you don't risk anything, you can risk even more."

Erica Jong
1942
American Writer

"Superior people never make long visits."

Marianne Moore
1887 - 1972
American Poet

"The battle to keep up appearances unnecessarily, the mask—whatever name you give creeping perfectionism— robs us of our energies."

Robin Worthington
1932
American Writer

"There's a period of life when we swallow a knowledge of ourselves and it becomes either good or sour inside."

Pearl Bailey
1918 - 1990
American Singer

"Laziness may appear attractive, but work gives satisfaction."

Anne Frank
1929 - 1945
German Diarist

Jane Addams was an American social reformer and pacifist, who won the Nobel Prize for Peace in 1931.

She is probably best known as the founder of Hull House, Chicago, one of the first social settlements in North America. A boarding club for working girls, Hull House offered college-level courses in various subjects and instruction in art, music and crafts. In addition to services and cultural opportunities for the largely immigrant population, Hull House trained young social workers in the practical aspects of the field.

Addams worked with labor and other reform groups for the first juvenile court law, tenement house regulations, an eight hour working day for women, factory inspection and worker's compensation.

In 1910 she became the first woman president of the National Conference of Social Work, and in 1912 she took an active part in the Progressive Party's presidential campaign for Theodore Roosevelt.

Jane Addams committed her life to justice for immigrants and blacks, equal rights for women and to the struggle against poverty in the United States.

JANE ADDAMS
1860 - 1935

" *Unless* our conception of patriotism is progressive, it cannot hope to embody the real affection and the real interest of the nation."

"... *The* fruitful processes of cooperation in the great experiment of living together in a world become conscious of itself."

" *In* his own way each man must struggle, lest the normal law become a far off abstraction utterly separated from his active life."

" *Civilization* is a method of living, an attitude of equal respect for all men."

JANE ADDAMS
1860 - 1935

*A*merican anthropologist Margaret Meads'
great fame owed as much to the force of her personality and
outspokenness as it did to the quality of her scientific work.

As an anthropologist, she was best known for her studies
of the non-literate peoples of Oceania, especially with regard to
various aspects of psychology and culture, the cultural
conditioning of sexual behavior, natural character and
culture change.

As a celebrity, she was widely known for her forays into
such far-ranging topics as women's rights, childbearing, sexual
morality, nuclear proliferation, race relations, drug abuse,
population control, environmental pollution and world hunger.

Elected to the presidency of the American Association for the
Advancement of Science at the age of 72, Margaret Mead
dedicated herself to an understanding of the origins and
continuing development of humanity.

MARGARET MEAD
1901 - 1978

"*We* are living beyond our means. As a people we have developed a life-style that is draining the earth of its priceless and irreplaceable resources without regard for the future of our children and people all around the world."

"*If* we are to achieve a richer culture, rich in contrasting values, we must recognize the whole gamut of human potentialities, and so weave a less arbitrary social fabric, one in which each diverse human gift will find a fitting place."

"*One* of the oldest human needs is having someone to wonder where you are, when you don't come home at night."

"*A* society which is clamoring for choice, which is filled with many articulate groups, each urging its own brand of salvation, its own variety of economic philosophy, will give each new generation no peace until all have chosen or gone under, unable to bear the conditions of choice. The stress is in our civilization."

MARGARET MEAD
1901 - 1978

"*I have crossed over on the backs of Sojourner Truth, Harriet Tubman, Fannie Lou Hamer and Madam C. J. Walker. Because of them I can now live the dream. I am the seed of the free, and I know it. I intend to bear great fruit.*"

Oprah Winfrey
1954
American Actress
and Television Talk Show Host

"*Matter and death are mortal illusions.*"

Mary Baker Eddy
1821-1910
Founder of the Christian Science Religion

"*I do not believe in sex distinction in literature, law, politics, or trade—or that modesty and virtue are more becoming to women than men.*"

Belva Lockwood
1830-1917
First Woman to Practice Law
before the Supreme Court

"*It's a fact that it is much more comfortable to be in the position of the person who has been offended than to be the unfortunate cause of it.*"

Barbara Walters
1931
American Journalist, Writer,
Television Producer and Commentator

"*We are not interested in the possibilities of defeat.*"

Queen Victoria
1819 - 1901
Queen of Great Britain

"*The most exciting thing about women's liberation is that this century will be able to take advantage of talent and potential genius that have been wasted because of taboos.*"

Helen Reddy
1941
Australian/American Singer and Songwriter

"*It's odd that you can get so anesthetized by your own pain or your own problem that you don't quite fully share the hell of someone close to you.*"

Lady Bird Johnson
1912
Former First Lady of the United States

"*We are concerned not only about the Negro poor, but the poor all over America and all over the world. Every man deserves a right to a job or an income so that he can pursue liberty, life, and happiness.*"

Coretta Scott King
1927
American Lecturer, Writer, and Civil Rights Activist

A United States medical physicist, Rosalyn Sussman Yalow was awarded a share of the 1977 Nobel Prize for Medicine for her development of a procedure called radioimmunoassay (RIA).

While a consultant in nuclear physics for the Bronx Veterans Administration Hospital during the late 1940's, she began investigating various medical applications of radioactive isotopes. By combining techniques from radioisotope tracing and immunology, Yalow developed RIA. The technique proved to be a very sensitive and simple means for measuring minute concentrations of biological and pharmacological substances in blood or other fluid samples. RIA was first applied in studying insulin concentrations in the blood of diabetics, but soon found hundreds of other applications.

In 1976, Rosalyn Sussman Yalow became the first woman to be awarded the Albert Lasker Prize for basic medical research.

ROSALYN SUSSMAN YALOW
1921

"*The* failure of women to have reached positions of leadership has been due in large part to social and professional discrimination."

~ ~ ~

"*We* cannot expect in the immediate future that all women who seek it will achieve full equality of opportunity. But if women are to start moving towards that goal, we must believe in ourselves; we must match our aspirations with the competence, courage and determination to succeed."

~ ~ ~

"*In* the past, few women have tried and even fewer have succeeded."

~ ~ ~

"*We* still live in a world in which a significant fraction of people, including women, believe that a woman belongs and wants to belong exclusively in the home."

ROSALYN SUSSMAN YALOW
1921

*"Don't compromise yourself.
You are all you've got."*

Janis Joplin
1943 - 1970
American Singer and Songwriter

*"Happiness, I do not know where to
turn to discover you on earth,
in the air or the sky; yet I know
you exist and are no futile dream."*

Rosalía de Castro
1837 - 1885
Spanish Novelist and Poet

"A closed mind is a dying mind."

Edna Ferber
1887 - 1968
Playwright and Novelist

*"Almsgiving tends to perpetuate
poverty; aid does away with it once and
for all. Almsgiving leaves a man just where
he was before. Aid restores him to society
as an individual worthy of all respect and
not as a man with a grievance."*

Eva Perón
1919 - 1952
Argentinean Politician, Government Official
and Lecturer

"We all live with the objective of being happy; our lives are all different and yet the same."

Anne Frank
1929 - 1945
German Diarist

"Art is not for the cultivated taste. It is to cultivate taste."

Nikki Giovanni
1943
American Poet, Author, and Lecturer

"I'm having trouble managing the mansion. What I need is a wife."

Ella Tambussi Grasso
1919
First Woman to become a
State Governor in her own right

"There is a spirit and a need and a man at the beginning of every great human advance. Every one of these must be right for that particular moment of history, or nothing happens."

Coretta Scott King
1927
American Lecturer, Writer, and Civil Rights Activist

*G*rowing up in Montgomery, Alabama,
Rosa Parks quickly gained firsthand experience with
prejudice and inequality. For years she lived with the
knowledge that blacks in the South were not entitled to the
same rights as those in the North.

In 1955, when Rosa Parks refused to give up her seat on
a Montgomery bus to a white man, her defiance ignited a
bus boycott of 381 days. Rosa Park's action gave thousands
of people the courage to speak out against the injustice
toward Southern blacks, furthering the Civil Rights
Movement in America.

Rosa Parks continues to influence societal acceptance,
co-founding the Rosa and Raymond Parks Institute
for self-development in 1988.

ROSA PARKS
1913

*"I'm just an average citizen.
Many black people before me were
arrested for defying the bus laws.
They prepared the way."*

*"I've been dreaming, looking, for as far
back as I had any thought of what it should
be like to be a human being. My desires
were to be free as soon as I had learned that
there had been slavery of human beings and
that I was a descendant from them."*

*"Many whites, even white Southerners,
told me that even though it may have
seemed like the blacks were being freed,
they felt more free and at ease themselves."*

*"Whatever my individual desires were
to be free, I was not alone. There were
many others who felt the same way."*

ROSA PARKS
1913

"Anybody singing the blues is in a deep pit yelling for help."

Mahalia Jackson
1911 - 1972
American Gospel Singer

"No good deed goes unpunished."

Clare Boothe Luce
1903
American Diplomat, Congresswoman
and Government Official

"Careful grooming may take twenty years off a woman's age, but you can't fool a long flight of stairs."

Marlene Dietrich
1901 - 1992
German/American Actress and Singer

"To succeed is nothing, it's an accident. But to feel no doubts about oneself is something very different: it is character."

Marie Lenéru
1875 - 1940
French Writer and Playwright

"I would not be President because I do not aspire to be President but I'm sure that a woman will be President. When? I don't know. It depends. I don't think the woods are full of candidates today."

Ella Tambussi Grasso
1919
First Woman to become a
State Governor in her own right

"A man's home may seem to be his castle on the outside; inside it is more often his nursery."

Clare Boothe Luce
1903
American Diplomat, Congresswoman,
and Government Official

"Charity separates the rich from the poor; aid raises the needy and sets him on the same level with the rich."

Eva Perón
1919 - 1952
Argentine Politician, Government Official,
and Lecturer

"Life is what happens to you when you're making other plans."

Betty Talmadge
1924
American Food Broker

*Louisa May Alcott was an American author
known for her children's books. She spent most of her life in
Boston and Concord, Massachusetts, where she grew up in the
company of such literary greats as Ralph Waldo Emerson,
Theodore Parker and Henry David Thoreau.*

*Growing up in a Transcendentalist family, Alcott developed
a lifelong concern for the welfare of her family. As
a young women, she taught briefly and worked as a domestic
to help provide for her parents and three sisters.
Eventually, she began to write.*

*While a nurse during the Civil War, she contracted typhoid
from unsanitary hospital conditions and was sent home.
She was never completely well again, but the publication of her
letters in book form, Hospital Sketches (1863) brought her
first taste of fame. Her 1869 book, Little Women, was an
immediate success. The book described the domestic
adventures of a New England family of modest means but
optimistic outlook.*

*Louisa May Alcott published five other books based on
recollections of her childhood before her death in 1888.*

LOUISA MAY ALCOTT
1832 - 1888

"*Love* is the only thing that we can carry with us when we go, and it makes the end so easy."

～ ⁊ ～

"...*Love* is a great beautifier."

～ ⁊ ～

"*You* have a good many little gifts and virtues, but there is no need of parading them, for conceit spoils the finest genius. There is not much danger that real talent or goodness will be overlooked long, and the great charm of all power is modesty."

～ ⁊ ～

"*Far* away there in the sunshine are my highest aspirations. I may not reach them, but I can look up and see their beauty, believe in them, and try to follow where they lead."

LOUISA MAY ALCOTT
1832 - 1888

"*Why not seize the pleasure at once?
How often is happiness destroyed by
preparation, foolish preparation!*"

Jane Austen
1775 - 1817
English Writer

"*The respect that is only bought by gold
is not worth much.*"

Frances E. W. Harper
1825 - 1911
American Lecturer and Author

"*The one thing that doesn't abide
majority rule is a person's conscience.*"

Harper Lee
1926
American Writer and Pulitzer Prize Winner

"*For loneliness is but cutting adrift from
our moorings and floating out to the open
sea; an opportunity for finding ourselves,
our real selves, what we are about, where
we are heading during our little time on
this beautiful earth.*"

Anne Shannon Monroe
1877 - 1942
American Lecturer, Novelist and Journalist

"*No matter how old a mother is she watches her middle-aged children for signs of improvement.*"

Florida Scott-Maxwell
1883
American/Scottish Writer, Suffragist and Psychologist

"*I postpone death by living, by suffering, by error, by risking, by giving, by loving.*"

Anaïs Nin
1903 - 1985
French/American Writer and Lecturer

"*Think of ideas as a beat. To change a mind is to change the world.*"

Dean Joan Konner
American Journalist and College Administrator

"*You take people as far as they will go, not as far as you would like them to go.*"

Jeannette Rankin
1880 - 1973
American Pacifist, Suffragist and Congresswoman

A humanitarian and founder of the
American Red Cross, Clara Barton was known as
the "angel of the battlefield."

At the outbreak of the Civil War, she organized an agency to
obtain and distribute supplies for the relief of wounded soldiers.
In 1865, at the request of President Abraham Lincoln, she set
up a bureau of records to aid in the search for missing men.
While Barton was in Europe for a rest, she became associated
with the International Red Cross, and in 1881 she established
the American National Red Cross. The next year, she succeeded
in having the United States sign the Geneva Agreement on the
treatment of sick, wounded and dead in battle and the
handling of prisoners of war.

Clara Barton is responsible for the American amendment
to the constitution of the Red Cross, which provides for
the distribution of relief not only in war but in times
of such calamities as famines, floods, earthquakes,
cyclones and pestilence.

CLARA BARTON
1821 - 1912

"Everybody's business is nobody's business, and nobody's business is my business."

"It is wise statesmanship which suggests that in time of peace we must prepare for war, and it is no less a wise benevolence that makes preparation in the hour of peace for assuaging the ills that are sure to accompany war."

"An institution or reform movement that is not selfish, must originate in the recognition of some evil that is adding to the sum of human suffering, or diminishing the sum of happiness. I suppose it is a philanthropic movement to try to reverse the process."

CLARA BARTON
1821 - 1912

"Set the foot down with distrust on the crust of the world—it is thin."

Edna St. Vincent Millay
1892 - 1952
Poet, Playwright and Writer

"Art and religion first; then philosophy; lastly science. That is the order of the great subjects of life, that's their order of importance."

Muriel Spark
1918
Scottish Writer and Poet

"People who fight fire with fire usually end up with ashes."

Abigail Van Buren
1918
American Newspaper Columnist and Lecturer

"Don't be afraid to feel as angry or as loving as you can, because when you feel nothing, it's just death."

Lena Horne
1917
American Singer, Actress and recipient
of the Kennedy Center Lifetime Achievement Award

"Without fanaticism we cannot accomplish anything."

Eva Perón
1919 - 1952
Argentine Politician, Government Official and Lecturer

"The family is the building block for whatever solidarity there is in society."

Jill Ruckelshaus
1937
American Government Official and Lecturer

"Women and elephants never forget."

Dorothy Parker
1893 - 1967
American Writer and Poet

"I don't know anything about luck. I've never banked on it, and I'm afraid of people who do. Luck to me is something else: hard work—and realizing what is opportunity and what isn't."

Lucille Ball
1911 - 1989
American Actress and Comedienne

*S*hirley Chisholm is the first black woman to have been elected to the United States Congress. She served the 12th Congressional District of Brooklyn for seven terms from 1968 until 1982.

In 1972, Chisholm made an unprecedented bid for the Presidential nomination of the Democratic Party, when she received 158 delegate votes. The campaign came one year after she helped co-found the National Women's Political Caucus (NWPC). Designed to mobilize women's political power, the NWPC encourages women to run for political office and endorses those candidates of either sex who support women's rights. She also is the founder and chairwoman of the National Political Congress of Black Women.

In her convictions and courage, Shirley Chisholm lives true to the title of her 1970 autobiography, Unbought and Unbossed.

SHIRLEY CHISHOLM
1924

"*Tremendous amounts of talent are being lost to our society just because that talent wears a skirt.*"

❧

"*U.S. politics is a beautiful fraud that has been imposed on the people for years, whose practitioners exchange gilded promises for the most valuable thing their victims' own, their votes.*"

❧

"*There is little place in the political scheme of things for an independent, creative personality, for a fighter. Anyone who takes that role must pay a price.*"

❧

"*Most Americans have never seen the ignorance, degradation, hunger, sickness, and the futility in which many other Americans live...They won't become involved in economic or political change until something brings the seriousness of the situation home to them.*"

SHIRLEY CHISHOLM
1924

"When you put your hand to the plow, you can't put it down until you get to the end of the row."

Alice Paul
1885 - 1977
American Author of the Equal Rights Amendment

"As a woman I have no country. As a woman my country is the whole world."

Virginia Woolf
1882 - 1941
British Author

"Art is the only way to run away without leaving home."

Twyla Tharp
1941
American Choreographer

"Love has pride in nothing— but its own humility."

Clare Boothe Luce
1903
American Diplomat and Congresswoman

"You don't get to choose how you're going to die, or when. You can only decide how you're going to live. Now!"

Joan Baez
1941
American Folksinger and Civil Rights Activist

"There is no reason to repeat bad history."

Eleanor Holmes Norton
1937
American Lawyer and Civil Rights Leader

"Every generation must go further than the last or what's the use in it? A baker's son must bake better bread—a miner's son—each generation a mite further."

Wilhelmina Kemp Johnstone
1900
Bahamian Poet and Writer

"It's the friends you can call up at 4 A.M. that matter."

Marlene Dietrich
1901 - 1992
German Actress

*An American poet, Emily Dickinson is
recognized as one of the greatest poets of the 19th century.
Her verse, along with that of Emerson and Whitman, best
defines the distinctive qualities of the American experience.*

*Emily Dickinson lived intensely, finding in her books,
garden and friends the possibilities of rich experience
and fulfillment. After her father's death in 1874, she went
into the seclusion that led to her being called
"the nun of Amherst."*

*Over a thousand poems were discovered in Emily
Dickinson's bureau after her death. In all, she wrote nearly
1,800 poems, several hundred of which are among the finest
ever written by any American poet. She gave only 24
of the poems titles, and only seven were published
during her lifetime.*

EMILY DICKINSON
1830 - 1886

"*To live is so startling it leaves little time
for anything else.*"

~ ❦ ~

"*Success is counted sweetest by those
who ne'er succeed.*"

~ ❦ ~

"*Hope is the thing with feathers,
that perches in the soul, and sings the
tune without the words, and never
stops at all.*"

~ ❦ ~

"*If it makes my whole body so cold no
fire can warm me, I know it is poetry.*"

EMILY DICKINSON
1830 - 1886

" Opportunities are usually disguised by hard work so most people don't recognize them."

Ann Landers
1918
American Newspaper Columnist

"If I'd been a housemaid I'd have been the best in Australia—I couldn't help it. It's got to be perfection for me."

Dame Nellie Melba
1861 - 1931
Australian Opera Singer

"A happy woman is one who has no cares at all; a cheerful woman is one who has cares but doesn't let them get her down."

Beverly Sills
1929
American Opera Singer

"Trouble is a part of life, and if you don't share it, you don't give the person who loves you a chance to love you enough."

Dinah Shore
1920
American Singer and Actress

"Thoughts are energy, and you can make your world or break your world by your thinking."

Susan L. Taylor
1946
American Journalist

"The human mind can bear plenty of reality, but not too much unintermittent gloom."

Margaret Drabble
1939
English Writer

"The freer that women become, the freer will men be. Because when you enslave someone, you are enslaved."

Louise Nevelson
1900 - 1988
Russian/American Sculptor and Feminist

"The more I traveled the more I realized that fear makes strangers of people who should be friends."

Shirley MacLaine
1934
American Actress and Writer

*W*ell-known as one of the most forceful
and articulate campaigners for women's rights, Gloria Steinem
assumed the role of a feminist leader in the late 1960's.
A journalist, lecturer and television personality, she has used
her communication abilities to introduce the general public
to issues of the women's liberation movement.

Steinem's most ambitious project involved the 1972
launching of "Ms.", a non-traditional women's magazine
devoted to raising the consciousness of American women. The
Toledo, Ohio native also has been instrumental in founding or
directing associations to help end discrimination, such as the
National Organization of Women and National
Women's Political Caucus.

Through her tireless fundraising, writing
and public speaking efforts, Gloria Steinem remains
an active political and social critic.

GLORIA STEINEM
1936

"*The* first problem for all of us,
men and women, is not to learn, but
to unlearn."

∼ ✦ ∼

"*Intelligence* at the service of poor
instinct is really dangerous."

∼ ✦ ∼

"*The* new women in politics seem to be
saying that we already know how to lose,
thank you very much. Now we want to
learn how to win."

∼ ✦ ∼

"*I* have met brave women who are
exploring the outer edge of human
possibility, with no history to guide
them, and with a courage to make
themselves vulnerable that I find
moving beyond words."

GLORIA STEINEM
1936

"*Marriage is a great institution—but I'm not ready for an institution yet.*"

Mae West
1892 - 1980
American Actress

"*It never occurred to me any more than to a man that I'd stop and turn off my mind because I had children. I think that because I had a strong feeling about what I wanted to do, it enabled me to continue. I never thought of it as unusual.*"

Sylvia Earle
1935
American Marine Biologist

"*God's gifts put man's best dreams to shame.*"

Elizabeth Barrett Browning
1806 - 1861
English Poet

"*The human heart yearns for the beautiful in all ranks of life.*"

Harriet Beecher Stowe
1811 - 1896
American Writer and Social Critic

"Sex appeal is fifty percent what you've got, and fifty percent what people think you've got."

Sophia Loren
1934
Italian Actress

"I believe in hard work. It keeps the wrinkles out of the mind and the spirit. It helps to keep a woman young."

Helena Rubinstein
1870 - 1965
American Businesswoman and
Founder of the Helena Rubinstein Company

"In Hollywood, all marriages are happy. It's trying to live together afterwards that causes problems."

Shelley Winters
1922
American Actress

"The world is round and the place which may seem like the end, may also be only the beginning."

Ivy Baker Priest
1905 - 1975
United States Secretary of the Treasury

A United States sportswoman, Babe Didrikson Zaharias was one of the greatest women athletes, a remarkable performer in basketball, track and field, and golf.

In 1930 and 1931, she was a member of the women's All-America basketball team. At the 1932 Olympic Games, she won the 80-meter hurdles and the javelin throw, and was deprived of a third gold medal only because she had used the then unorthodox Western roll in winning the high jump. Zaharias also excelled in baseball, softball, swimming, figure skating, billiards and even football.

She began to golf casually in 1932, but from 1934 on she (dedicated herself to the game). Restored to amateur status after several years as a professional, she won the U.S. Women's Amateur tournament in 1946.

Known as much for her skill as her determination, Babe Didrickson Zaharias opened the door to the male-dominated domain of sports.

BABE DIDRIKSON ZAHARIAS
1914 - 1956

"All of my life I've always had the urge to do things better than anybody else."

"All of my life I've been competing and competing to win."

"I don't seem able to do my best unless I'm behind or in trouble."

"That little white ball won't move until you hit it, and there's nothing you can do after it has gone."

BABE DIDRIKSON ZAHARIAS
1914 - 1956

"A sphere is not made up of one, but of an infinite number of circles; women have diverse gifts and to say that women's sphere is the family circle is a mathematical absurdity."

Maria Mitchell
1818 - 1889
First Woman Astronomer in the United States and the
First Woman member of the American Academy
of Arts and Sciences, Hall of Fame

"In real love you want the other person's good. In romantic love you want the other person."

Margaret Anderson
1893 - 1973
American Writer

"I crusaded for women as well as all ethics in the church. Our proclamation and resolutions are great. We have yet to live them out."

Leontine T. C. Kelly
1920
First Black Woman Bishop of a
Religion in the United States

"You can't be brave if you've only had wonderful things happen to you."

Mary Tyler Moore
1937
American Actress

"Let the world know you as you are, not as you think you should be, because sooner or later, if you are posing, you will forget the pose, and then where are you?"

Fannie Brice
1891 - 1951
American Comedienne and Singer

"I like not only to be loved, but to be told that I am loved; the realm of silence is large enough beyond the grave."

George Eliot
1819 - 1880
English Writer

"Marrying a man is like buying something you've been admiring for a long time in a shop window. You may love it when you get it home, but it doesn't always go with everything else in the house."

Jean Kerr
1923
American Playwright

"In passing, also, I would like to say that the first time Adam had a chance he laid the blame on a woman."

Nancy Astor
1879 - 1964
British Politician

*In 1849, Elizabeth Blackwell became the first
woman in the United States to become a physician. Determined
to learn the intricacies of medicine, she studied privately after
being refused admittance to several medical schools.
Finally, Geneva Medical College in New York accepted
her as a student in 1847.*

*As a young doctor, Blackwell raised funds to open a hospital
for needy women and children. During the Civil War, she
trained nurses for the Union Army and, in 1868, opened a
medical school for women. In 1875, she co-founded a school of
medicine for women in England and later spent her retirement
years writing medical books.*

*A self-made and courageous woman, Elizabeth Blackwell was a
pioneer in the education of women as physicians.*

ELIZABETH BLACKWELL
1821 - 1910

"*I must have something to engross my thoughts, some object in life which will fill this vacuum and prevent this sad wearing away of the heart.*"

"*It is not easy to be a pioneer—but oh, it is fascinating! I would not trade one moment; even the worst moment, for all the riches in the world.*"

"*Medicine is so broad a field, so closely interwoven with general interests, dealing as it does with all ages, sexes, and classes, and yet of so personal a character in its individual applications, that it must be regarded as one of those great departments of work in which the cooperation of men and women is needed to fulfill all its requirements.*"

"*For what is done or learned by one class of women becomes, by virtue of their common womanhood, the property of all women.*"

ELIZABETH BLACKWELL
1821 - 1910

*"Faith is the subtle chain which binds us
to the infinite."*

Elizabeth Oakes Smith
1806 - 1893
American Writer, Lecturer and Social Reformer

*"I hope we can pay teachers the salaries
that they deserve. It is absolutely fantastic
that we have given such a poor status level
to the most important shapers of human
character and development we have in
this country."*

Jewel Plummer Cobb
1924
American Biologist and
President of California State University

*"Whoever loves true life,
will love true love."*

Elizabeth Barret Browning
1806 - 1861
English Poet

*"I say that if each person in this world
will simply take a small piece of this huge
thing, this tablecloth, bedspread,
whatever, and work it regardless
of the color of the yarn, we will have
harmony on this planet."*

Cicely Tyson
1933
American Actress

"I came from a poor and humble background. I did not come from a family of people who had a poverty view of the world. I came from people who viewed the world as attainable."

Faye Wattleton
1943
American Nurse and Former President of the
Planned Parenthood Federation of America

"We are laying the foundation for children to build on. We tried to build in them dependability and responsibility."

Rudy Middleton Forsythe
1905
American Teacher for over sixty years in a one-room
schoolhouse in South Carolina

"I was always looking outside myself for strength and confidence but it comes from within. It is there all the time."

Anna Freud
1895 - 1982
Austrian Psychotherapist
and the daughter of Sigmund Freud

"If you banish fear, nothing terribly bad can happen to you."

Margaret Bourke-White
1906 - 1971
American Photographer

*An author noted for her novels of life in China,
Pearl S. Buck was the recipient of the Nobel Prize for Literature
in 1938. She spent her youth in China, where her parents were
Presbyterian missionaries.*

*Buck received her early education in Shanghai and returned to
teach at a Chinese university after graduating from a Virginia
womens' college in 1914. Her articles and stories about Chinese
life first appeared in U.S. magazines in 1923, but it was not
until 1931 that she reached a wide audience with* The Good
Earth. *The unique story described the struggle of a Chinese
peasant and his slave-wife to gain land and position.*

*After World War II, in a move to aid illegitimate children of
U.S. servicemen in Asian countries, she instituted the
Pearl S. Buck Foundation. To this organization she donated
more than $7 million of her personal earnings.*

*Living to write and living a life worth writing about, Pearl S.
Buck changed the way people viewed other areas of the world.*

PEARL   S.   BUCK
1892 - 1973

"Every great mistake has a halfway moment, a split second when it can be recalled and perhaps remedied."

"Hunger makes a thief of any man."

"One faces the future with one's past."

"When hope is taken away from the people moral degeneration follows swiftly after."

PEARL S. BUCK
1892 - 1973

"*The only reason I would take up jogging is so that I could hear heavy breathing again.*"

Erma Bombeck
1927
American Humorist and Writer

"*One's old acquaintances sometimes come upon one like ghosts—and most people hate ghosts.*"

Margaret Baillie Saunders
1873 - 1949
English Writer

"*I think success has no rules, but you can learn a great deal from failure.*"

Jean Kerr
1923
American Playwright

On receiving the Nobel Prize, "It might seem unfair to reward a person for having so much pleasure over the years, asking the maize plant to solve specific problems and then watching its responses. I can't imagine a better life."

Barbara McClintoch
1902
American Geneticist and the First Woman to receive the
Nobel Prize in medicine without a collaborator

*"Measure not the work until the day's
out and the labor done."*

Elizabeth Barret Browning
1806 - 1861
English Poet

*"You must learn to be still in the midst
of activity, and to be vibrantly
alive in repose."*

Indira Gandhi
1917 - 1984
Prime Minister of India

*"In my younger days, when I was pained
by the half-educated, loose and inaccurate
ways women had, I used to say, 'How
much women need exact science.' But
since I have known some workers in
science, I have now said, 'How much
science needs women.'"*

Maria Mitchell
1818 - 1889
First Woman Astronomer in the United States and the
First Woman member of the American Academy
of Arts and Sciences, Hall of Fame

*"The environment that people live in is
the environment that they learn to live in,
respond to, and perpetuate. If the
environment is good, so be it. But if it is
poor, so is the quality of life within it."*

Ellen Swallow Richards
1842 - 1911
American Chemist and Ecologist

Indian leader Sarah Winnemucca was a Pauite chief in Nevada. Both her father and grandfather preceded her as chiefs of this great American tribe.

For years, Winnemucca labored, speaking out on the poor living conditions and abusive handling of Indians under United States policy. She lobbied Congress to improve the situation of her people. Chief Winnemucca carried her cause across the country lecturing and writing on the difficult plight of all Indian nations. Her endless efforts resulted in a governmental grant approving Indian land use in Nevada.

For her tireless dedication to Indian rights, Sarah Winnemucca will forever stand out as a hero of her people.

SARAH WINNEMUCCA
1844 - 1891

"*If you make fun of bad persons you make yourself beneath them...Be kind to bad and good, for you don't know your own heart.*"

~ ⊗ ~

"*The saddest day hath gleams of light,
The darkest wave hath bright foam beneath it,
The twinkles o'er the cloudiest night,
Some solitary star to cheer it.*"

~ ⊗ ~

"*Nobody really knows Indians who cheat them and treat them badly.*"

~ ⊗ ~

"*No man can be a leader among Indians who is not a good man.*"

SARAH WINNEMUCCA
1844 - 1891

"*The point of nonviolence is to build a floor, a strong new floor, beneath which we can no longer sink.*"

Joan Baez
1941
American Folksinger and Civil Rights Activist

"*You have to sniff out joy; keep your nose to the joy-trail.*"

Buffy Sainte-Marie
1941
Canadian Songwriter, Singer and the Founder of the
North American Women's Association

"*The suburbs were discovered, quite by accident, one day in the early 1940's by a Welcome Wagon lady who was lost.*"

Erma Bombeck
1927
American Humorist and Writer

"*The first idea that a child must acquire in order to be actively disciplined is that of the difference between good and evil; and the task of the educators lies in seeing that a child does not confound good with immobility, and evil with activity.*"

Maria Montessori
1870 - 1952
Italian Educator and the Founder of Montessori Schools

"I am angry at the condition of a society that creates problems for blacks and for women. But I think there are ways anger can be turned into something positive."

Jewel Plummer Cobb
1924
American Biologist and
President of California State University

"Independence I have long considered the grand blessing of life, the basis of every virtue."

Mary Wollstonecraft
1759 - 1797
American Feminist

"For fast-acting relief try slowing down."

Lily Tomlin
1936
American Comedienne and Actress

"All times are beautiful for those who manage joy within them; but there is no happy or favourable time for those with disconsolate or orphaned souls."

Rosalía de Castro
1837 - 1885
Spanish Novelist and Poet

One of 22 children, Wilma Rudolph
grew up in Tennessee. Stricken with polio at an early age,
Wilma believed she would one day walk again without braces
because of her mother's inspiration.

At the age of nine, the braces were removed and Rudolph spent
all of her free time running and at play. In the years that
followed, she was extremely active in basketball and track.

Rudolph excelled as an athlete, and her years of dedication
were rewarded in 1960 at the Olympic Games in Rome. She
was the first woman to win three gold medals in track and field.

Today, Wilma Rudolph passes on her skill and determination
as the Track Director and Special Consultant on Minority
Affairs at DePauw University, Greencastle, Indiana.

WILMA RUDOLPH
1940

"*My* mother was the one who made me
work, made me believe that one day
it would be possible for me to walk
without braces."

I've been asked to run as a pro, but my
interests now are my family...and the kids
I'm working with. Now I'm trying to
develop other champions."

"*I* would be very disappointed if I were
only remembered as a runner because I
feel that my contribution to the youth of
America has far exceeded the woman
who was the Olympic champion.
The challenge is still there."

"*S*ometimes it takes years to really grasp
what has happened to your life."

WILMA RUDOLPH
1940

*"I've always been proud of my age.
I think people should be proud
they've been around long enough to
have learned something."*

Frances Moore Lappé
American Author

*"We'll make a space in the lives that we
planned and here I'll stay until it's time
for you to go."*

Buffy Sainte-Marie
1941
Canadian Songwriter, Singer and the Founder of the
North American Women's Association

*"What a strange thing is memory, and
hope; one looks backward, the other
forward. The one is of today, the other is of
tomorrow. Memory is history recorded in
our brain, memory is a painter, it paints
pictures of the past and of the day."*

Grandma Moses
1860 - 1961
American Painter

*"Remember, Ginger Rogers did
everything Fred Astaire did, but she did it
backwards and in high heels."*

Faith Whittlesey
1939
Lawyer and Diplomat

"My life has been a tapestry of rich and royal hue, an everlasting vision of the everchanging view."

Carole King
1941
American Singer and Songwriter

"People are just not very ambitious for women still. Your son you want to be the best he can be. Your daughter you want to be happy."

Aexa Canady
1950
First Black Woman Neurosurgeon in the United States

"If you haven't forgiven yourself something, how can you forgive others?"

Dolores Huerta
1930
Vice President of the United Farm Workers of America

"Everybody wants to do something to help, but nobody wants to be first."

Pearl Bailey
1918 - 1990
American Singer

*Katharine Hepburn, as a young woman,
became an instant success on the American stage
and in motion pictures. From the start, she was a spirited
performer with a touch of Yankee eccentricity. Unafraid of
challenges, Hepburn has commonly taken
courageous political stands and accepted roles that test her
acting ability. She introduced into film a strength of
character previously considered undesirable in Hollywood
leading ladies. A role model for women throughout
the world, she is noted for her brisk New England accent,
unique style and rare beauty.
Winner of four Academy Awards®, Katharine Hepburn
is a witty, independent woman who remains one of
the most beloved actresses in America.*

KATHARINE HEPBURN
1909

"*I* can remember walking as a child. It
was not customary to say you were
fatigued. It was customary to complete the
goal of the expedition."

~ ❧ ~

"*W*ithout discipline, there's no life at all."

~ ❧ ~

"*P*lain women know more about men
than beautiful ones do."

~ ❧ ~

"*T*o keep your character intact you
cannot stoop to filthy acts. It makes it
easier to stoop the next time."

KATHARINE HEPBURN
1909

"Farewell to thee, farewell to thee, thou charming one who dwells among the bowers, one fond embrace before I now depart until we meet again."

Lydia Kamekeha Liliuokalani
1838 - 1917
Queen of the Hawaiian Islands

"Some people are moulded by their admirations, others by their hostilities."

Elizabeth Bowen
1899 - 1973
Anglo/Irish Author

"For women there are, undoubtedly, great difficulties in the path, but so much the more to overcome. First, no woman should say, 'I am but a woman!' But a woman! What more can you ask to be?"

Maria Mitchell
1818 - 1889
First Woman Astronomer in the United States and the
First Woman member of the American Academy
of Arts and Sciences, Hall of Fame

"Had there been no difficulties and no thorns in the way, then man would have been in his primitive state and no progress made in civilization and mental culture."

Anandabai Joshee
1865 - 1887
Indian Physician

"*The trouble with the rat race is that even if you win, you're still a rat.*"

Lily Tomlin
1936
American Comedienne and Actress

"*Never turn down a job because you think it's too small, you don't know where it can lead.*"

Julia Morgan
1872 - 1957
American Architect

"*Creativity is not a driving force. It happens. It creates itself and you have to be open.*"

Mayumi Oda
Japanese Writer and Artist

"*My current view of the world is that life is braided streams of light and darkness, joy and pain, and I just accept them. They both exist and I walk them both. But now I know there is a choice about what I do with them.*"

Arisika Razak
Interpretive Dancer

Maine native, Margaret Chase Smith began her political career in 1930, when at the age of 33 she became a member of the Republican State Committee.

In 1940, Smith was elected to the Seventy-Seventh Congress. Her work as an advocate for female status in the military while on the House Naval Affairs Committee earned her the title, "Mother of the Waves." The independent-thinking Congresswoman from Maine served eight years in the House of Representatives until she was elected to the U.S. Senate in 1948.

Margaret Chase Smith's honest, straightforward way gained her widespread popularity across the country and serious consideration to be America's first female vice presidential candidate.

MARGARET CHASE SMITH
1897

"*I* believe that in our constant search for security we can never gain any peace of mind until we secure our own soul."

~ ❧ ~

"*My* creed is that public service must be more than doing a job efficiently and honestly. It must be a complete dedication to the people and to the nation with full recognition that every human being is entitled to courtesy and consideration, that constructive criticism is not only to be expected but sought, that smears are not only to be expected but fought, honor is to be earned but not bought."

~ ❧ ~

"*The* key to security is public information."

~ ❧ ~

"*Before* you can become a statesman you first have to get elected, and to get elected you have to be a politician pledging support for what the voters want."

MARGARET CHASE SMITH
1897

"*There is hope if people will begin to awaken that spiritual part of themselves— that heartfelt acknowledgement that we are the caretakers of life on this planet.*"

Brooke Medicine Eagle
American Indian Writer and Teacher

"*I think that education is power. I think that being able to communicate with people is power. One of my main goals on the planet is to encourage people to empower themselves.*"

Oprah Winfrey
1954
American Actress and Television Talk Show Host

"*To me success means effectiveness in the world, that I am able to carry my ideas and values into the world—that I am able to change it in positive ways.*"

Maxine Hong Kingston
Writer and Professor

"*I am convinced that we must train not only the head, but the heart and hand as well.*"

Madame Chiang Kai-shek
1898
Chinese Sociologist

"The critical responsibility for the generation you're in is, to help provide the shoulders, the direction, and the support for those generations who come behind."

Gloria Dean Randle Scott
1938
President of Bennett College, North Carolina

"Music has been my playmate, my lover and my crying towel. It gets me off like nothing else."

Buffy Sainte-Marie
1941
Canadian Songwriter, Singer and the Founder of the North American Women's Association

"In society it is etiquette for ladies to have the best chairs and get handed things. In the home the reverse is the case. That is why ladies are more sociable than gentlemen."

Virginia Graham
1912
American Writer and Playwright

"It's so clear that you have to cherish everyone. I think that's what I get from these older black women, that every soul is to be cherished, that every flower is to bloom."

Alice Walker
1944
Novelist and Winner of the Pulitzer Prize for Fiction

In the early 1960's, Mary Kay Ash did a makeover of American women. Forming the cosmetics company that bears her name, she created career options for women who had never worked out of the home. Ash's objective for direct selling beauty products: to give women the opportunity to "do anything they were smart enough to do."

Mary Kay Cosmetics has grown from nine consultants and revenues of $200,000 in its first year of operation to a multi-million dollar international organization. Throughout the tremendous growth, the company founder and chairwoman has been honored and recognized for her executive accomplishments and contributions to female independence.

Entrepreneurial and innovative, Mary Kay Ash is one of America's most dynamic businesswomen.

MARY KAY ASH

"*Aerodynamically the bumble bee shouldn't be able to fly, but the bumble bee doesn't know it, so it goes on flying anyway.*"

"Most people live and die with their music still unplayed. They never dare to try."

"A good goal is like a strenuous exercise—it makes you stretch."

"For every failure, there's an alternative course of action. You just have to find it. When you come to a roadblock, take a detour."

MARY KAY ASH

"*The first rule in opera is the first rule in life; see to everything yourself.*"

Dame Nellie Melba
1861 - 1931
Australian Opera Singer

"*Cleaning your house while your kids are still growing is like shoveling the walk before it stops snowing.*"

Phyllis Diller
1917
American Comedienne

"*This became a credo of mine... attempt the impossible in order to improve your work.*"

Bette Davis
1908 - 1991
American Actress

"*The first step toward liberation for any group is to use the power in hand...And the power in hand is the vote.*"

Helen Gahagan Douglas
1900 - 1980
American Congresswoman and Lecturer

*"We've got to work to save our
children and do it with full respect
for the fact that if we do not, no one else is
going to do it."*

Dorothy Irene Height
1912
President of the National Council of Negro Women

*"I love my past. I love my present. I'm
not ashamed of what I've had, and I'm not
sad because I have it no longer."*

Colette
1873 - 1954
French Writer

*"Life is a process of becoming, a
combination of states we have to go
through. Where people fail is that they
wish to elect a state and remain in it.
This is a kind of death."*

Anaïs Nin
1903 - 1985
French/American Writer and Lecturer

*"Believe only half of what you see and
nothing that you hear."*

Dinah Mulock Craik
1826 - 1887
Victorian Writer and Poet

*W*ilma Pearl Mankiller spent her early years
on a Cherokee farm in Oklahoma, where she first became
concerned with the mistreatment of the Cherokee Nation.

An activist for Indian rights, Mankiller believed that the
Cherokees themselves knew how best to resolve their own
problems. She worked with the Indian people to improve living
conditions and create opportunity.

Mankiller became the first woman deputy chief and, in 1985,
the Principal Chief of the Cherokee Nation. Today she governs
120,000 people of the second largest Indian nation
in the United States.

Promoting education, jobs and farming, Chief Wilma
Mankiller's determined way is restoring Cherokee communities.

WILMA PEARL MANKILLER
1945

"A lot of young girls have looked to their career paths and have said they'd like to be chief. There's been a change in the limits people see."

❧

She likened her job to "running a small country, a medium corporation, and being a social worker."

❧

"I've run into more discrimination as a woman than as an Indian."

❧

"I want to be remembered as the person who helped us restore faith in ourselves."

WILMA PEARL MANKILLER
1945

"Mistakes are a fact of life. It is the response to error that counts."

Nikki Giovanni
1943
American Poet

"We have always been trained in the past to a life of service and I am afraid that as these new changes come about there may be a loss of real values."

Empress Nagako
1903
Japanese Empress

"'Tis the motive exalts the action; 'Tis the doing, and not the deed."

Margaret Preston
1820 - 1897
American Poet and Writer

"Friendship of a kind that cannot easily be reversed tomorrow must have its roots in common interests and shared beliefs."

Barbara Tuchman
1912 - 1989
American Historian and Pulitzer Prize Winner

"If our American way of life fails the child, it fails us all."

Pearl S. Buck
1892 - 1973
American Author and recipient of the
Nobel Prize for Literature in 1938

"I am for lifting everyone off the social bottom. In fact, I am for doing away with the social bottom altogether."

Clare Boothe Luce
1903
American Diplomat and Congresswoman

"We live in the present, we dream of the future, but we learn eternal truths from the past."

Madame Chiang Kai-shek
1898
Chinese Sociologist

"Until I feared I would lose it, I never loved to read. One does not love breathing."

Harper Lee
1926
American Writer and Pulitzer Prize Winner

An American author, Margaret Mitchell was raised in Georgia. As the daughter of the president of the Atlanta Historical Society, she developed an intense interest in local history.

From this background, Mitchell started to write a novel of the Civil War and Reconstruction from a Southern point of view, transforming the stories she remembered from her childhood. After ten years and over 1,000 pages, Gone With the Wind was published in 1935. The novel won the Pulitzer Prize and the National Book Award. Gone With the Wind set a record in publishing history, selling 50,000 copies in one day. It has been translated into 30 languages.

Margaret Mitchell will be remembered for the book behind one of the most popular films ever made.

MARGARET MITCHELL
1900 - 1949

"*Life's* under no obligation to give us what we expect. We take what we get and are thankful it's no worse than it is."

～ ～ ～

"*Until* you've lost your reputation, you never realize what a burden it was or what freedom really is."

～ ～ ～

"*What* most people don't seem to realize is that there is just as much money to be made out of the wreckage of civilization as from the upbuilding of one."

～ ～ ～

"*Death* and taxes and childbirth! There's never any convenient time for any of them!"

MARGARET MITCHELL
1900 - 1949

*"Anger repressed can poison
a relationship as surely as the
cruelest words."*

Joyce Brothers
1925
American Psychologist and Journalist

*"It's the good girls who keep the diaries,
the bad girls never have the time."*

Tallulah Bankhead
1903 - 1968
American Actress

*"Never go to bed mad.
Stay up and fight."*

Phyllis Diller
1917
American Comedienne

*"Character contributes to beauty. It
fortifies a woman as her youth fades. A
mode of conduct, a standard of courage,
discipline, fortitude and integrity can do a
great deal to make a woman beautiful."*

Jacqueline Bisset
1946
English Actress

"*The* oppressed never free themselves—
they do not have the necessary strengths."

Clare Boothe Luce
1903
American Diplomat and Congresswoman

"*Take* each good day and relish
each moment. Take each bad day and
work to make it good."

Lisa Dado
1930
American Writer

"*I* don't want to live—I want to love
first, and live incidentally."

Zelda Fitzgerald
1900 - 1948
American Writer and Adventuress

"*A* woman today has to do more than
her male counterpart. Come in knowing
that you're going to have to give 200
percent effort to get 100 percent credit.
And most of the time you will get
100 percent credit."

Sherian Grace Codoria
1940
Brigadier General, highest-ranking Black Woman in the
United States Armed Forces and one of only four
female Army Generals

*An English nurse, Florence Nightingale
was the founder of trained nursing for women.*

*While in charge of nursing at a Turkish military hospital
during the Crimean War (1854 - 1856), she coped with
overcrowding, poor sanitation and a shortage of basic
medical supplies. As Nightingale made her nightly hospital
rounds she gave comfort and advice, establishing the image
of "The Lady with the Lamp" among the wounded.*

*Regarded as an expert on public hospitals, she was
dedicated to improving the health and living conditions of
the British soldier. In 1860, she founded the Nightingale
School for Nurses, the first such school of its kind
in London and the world.*

*Florence Nightingale has been immortalized as the
epitome of tender care.*

FLORENCE NIGHTINGALE
1820 - 1910

"*I* never lose an opportunity of urging a practical beginning, however small, for it is wonderful how often the mustard-seed germinates and roots itself."

"*I* stand at the altar of the murdered men, and while I live, I fight their cause."

"*I* can stand out the war with any man."

"*For* what is Mysticism? Is it not the attempt to draw near to God, not by rites or ceremonies but by inward disposition? Is it not merely a hard word for 'The kingdom of heaven is within'? Heaven is neither a place nor a time."

FLORENCE NIGHTINGALE
1820 - 1910

"If we get a government that reflects more of what this country is really about, we can turn the century – and the economy – around."

Bella Abzug
1920
American Congresswoman and Lawyer

"The will to be totally rational is the will to be made out of glass and steel: and to use others as if they were glass and steel."

Marge Piercy
1936
Founder of the Movement for a Democratic Society

"One of the indispensable foods of the human soul is liberty. Liberty, taking the word in its concrete sense, consists in the ability to choose."

Simone Weil
1910 - 1943
French Theologian, Philosopher, Journalist and Scholar

"Whoever said, 'It's not whether you win or lose that counts', probably lost."

Martina Navratilova
1956
Professional Tennis Player

"The more the wonders of the world become inaccessible, the more intensely do its curiosities affect us."

Colette
1873 - 1954
French Writer

"Honor wears different coats to different eyes."

Barbara Tuchman
1912 - 1989
American Historian and Pulitzer Prize Winner

"Like the resource it seeks to protect, wildlife conservation must be dynamic, changing as conditions change, seeking always to become more effective."

Rachel Carson
1907 - 1964
American Marine Biologist and Environmentalist

Discussing her relationship with Amelia Earhart—"We were united by common bond of interest. We spoke each other's language—and that was the language of pioneer women of the air."

Ruth Rowland Nichols
1901 - 1961
American Aviator and First Woman
to pilot a Passenger Airplane

A devoted and loving mother, Clara McBride Hale
raised her own children along with over 30 other
youngsters. Her unconditional love for children led this
remarkable woman to open Hale House in Harlem,
New York, during the early 1970's.

Hale House was a desperately needed center for infants
born to drug-addicted mothers. In the midst of poverty,
this program provided nurturing, love and medical
attention to those helpless babies of families who also
received care and rehabilitation. The legacy of this
extraordinary woman lives on in the current administrator
of the Hale House, Dr. Lorraine Hale, Clara McBride
Hale's daughter.

In 1985, "Mother" Clara McBride Hale was named an
"American hero" by President Ronald Reagan.

CLARA McBRIDE HALE
1905

"*Being* black does not stop you. You can sit out in the world and say, 'Well, white people kept me back, and I can't do this.' Not so. You can have anything you want if you make up your mind and you want it."

~ ❧ ~

"*Until* I die, I'm going to keep doing. My people need me. They need somebody that's not taking from them and is giving them something."

~ ❧ ~

"*When* I'm gone, somebody else will take it up and do it. This is how we've lived all these years."

~ ❧ ~

"*I'm* not an American hero. I'm a person who loves children."

CLARA McBRIDE HALE
1905

"Parents have become so convinced that educators know what is best for children that they forget that they themselves are really experts."

Marian Wright Edelman
1937
Founder of the Children's Defense Fund,
Civil Rights Activist and the First Black
Woman admitted to the bar in Mississippi

"In every out thrust headland, in every curving beach, in every grain of sand there is a story of the earth."

Rachel Carson
1907 - 1964
American Marine Biologist and Environmentalist

"Spirit is the real and eternal; matter is the unreal and temporal."

Mary Baker Eddy
1821 - 1910
Founder of the Christian Science Religion

"Clouds and darkness surround us, yet Heaven is just, and the day of triumph will surely come, when justice and truth will be vindicated. Our wrongs will be made right, and we will once more, taste the blessings of freedom."

Mary Todd Lincoln
1818 - 1882
Former First Lady of the United States

"My address is like my shoes. It travels with me. I abide where there is a fight against wrong."

Mother Jones
1830 - 1930
Irish/American Labor Organizer and Humanitarian

"Always the edge of the sea remains an elusive and indefinable boundary. The shore has a dual nature, changing with the swing of the tides, belonging now to the land, now to the sea."

Rachel Carson
1907 - 1964
American Marine Biologist and Environmentalist

"You have put me in here (jail) a cub, but I will come out roaring like a lion."

Carry Nation
1846 - 1911
American Prohibitionist

On physical love and labour: "labour: to feel with one's whole self the existence of the world. Love: to feel with one's whole self the existence of another being."

Simone Weil
1910 - 1943
French Theologian, Philosopher, Journalist and Scholar

*$\mathcal{R}$aised in New York, Elizabeth Cady Stanton
learned at a young age about discrimination against women.
She studied law with her father, Judge Daniel Cady, but was
refused admission to the bar because of her sex.*

*Angered by discrimination and legal restrictions against
women, Stanton became involved in antislavery and
temperance movements. In 1848, she was an organizer of the
Seneca Falls Convention, where she was the first to call for a
woman's right to vote. In 1851, Stanton convinced Susan B.
Anthony to join the women's rights movement. Together these
two women worked for female suffrage and expanded rights.*

*As president of the National Woman Suffrage Association,
Elizabeth Cady Stanton helped lay the foundation and
developed ideas which would become the platforms of the
women's rights movement.*

ELIZABETH CADY STANTON
1815 - 1902

"*Nothing strengthens the judgment and quickens the conscience like individual responsibility.*"

~ ~

"*To throw obstacles in the way of a complete education is like putting out the eyes.*"

~ ~

"*Reformers who are always compromising, have not yet grasped the idea that truth is the only safe ground to stand upon.*"

~ ~

"*I shall not grow conservative with age.*"

ELIZABETH CADY STANTON
1815 - 1902

" *We* are stardust. We are golden and we've got to get ourselves back to the garden."

Joni Mitchell
1943
American Singer and Songwriter

" *There* is only one real sin and that is to persuade oneself that the second— best, is anything but second best."

Doris Lessing
1919
English Author

" *The* country has suffered too much from its failure, generation after generation, to take on race, deal with it, and finally set it aside."

Eleanor Holmes Norton
1937
American Professor who was the First Woman to chair
the Equal Employment Opportunity Commission

" *I* think togetherness is a very important ingredient to family life. It's a cliché and we use it too much but I think for a husband and wife, the way to stay close is to do things together and to share."

Barbara Bush
1925
First Lady of the United States
and Humanitarian

"I deplore any action which denies artistic talent an opportunity to express itself because of prejudice against race origin."

Bess Truman
1885 - 1982
Former First Lady of the United States

"I don't mind if my life goes in the service of the nation. If I die, every drop of my blood will invigorate the nation."

Indira Gandhi
1917 - 1984
Prime Minister of India

"I felt a comedy ego beginning to grow, which gave me the courage to begin tentatively looking into myself for material."

Joan Rivers
1933
American Comedienne and Television Talk Show Host

"The legacy I want to leave is a child-care system that says that no kid is going to be left alone or left unsafe."

Marian Wright Edelman
1937
Founder of the Children's Defense Fund,
Civil Rights Activist and the First Black Woman
admitted to the bar in Mississippi

*A*n American aviator, Amelia Earhart was the first
woman to fly solo across the Atlantic Ocean.

After a Kansas upbringing and education, she learned to fly in
California, taking up aviation as a hobby. Following a series of
record flights, she made a solo transatlantic flight from Harbour
Grace, Newfoundland, to Ireland and later flew the first solo
from Hawaii to the American mainland.

In June 1937, Earhart attempted the first round-the-world flight
near the equator. After taking off on July 1 from New Guinea
for Howland Island in the Pacific, her plane vanished. A great
naval search failed to locate her and it was assumed that she
had been lost at sea.

The mystery and fascination surrounding Amelia Earhart's
life and death continue to the current day. The most current
research confirmed the discovery of portions of her aircraft on a
small remote island in the Pacific. There was, however,
no trace of any survivor.

AMELIA EARHART
1898 - 1937?

"*Courage is the price that life exacts for granting peace. The soul that knows it not, knows no release from little things.*"

"*In soloing—as in other activities— it is far easier to start something than to finish it.*"

"*There are two kinds of stones, as everyone knows, one of which rolls.*"

"*Adventure is worthwhile in itself.*"

AMELIA EARHART
1898 - 1937?

"I have great belief in the fact that whenever there is chaos, it creates wonderful thinking. I consider chaos a gift."

Septima Poinsette Clark
1898 - 1987
American Civil Rights Activist

"Boredom helps one to make decisions."

Colette
1873 - 1954
French Writer

"Something which we think is impossible now is not impossible in another decade."

Constance Baker Motley
1921
First Black Woman to become a
Federal Judge in the United States

"The ultimate goal should be doing your best and enjoying it."

Peggy Fleming
1948
American Athlete and Olympic Gold Medalist
in Ice Skating

"*The only causes of regret are laziness,
outbursts of temper, hurting others,
prejudice, jealousy and envy.*"

Germaine Greer
1939
Australian Author and Educator

"*If we could sell our experiences
for what they cost us,
we'd all be millionaires.*"

Abigail Van Buren
1918
American Newspaper Columnist and Lecturer

"*Expect trouble as an inevitable part
of life and repeat to yourself, the
most comforting words of all; This,
too, shall pass.*"

Ann Landers
1918
American Newspaper Columnist

"*The one thing that doesn't abide by
majority rule is a person's conscience.*"

Harper Lee
1926
American Writer and Pulitzer Prize Winner

*G*olda Meir was a founder of the State of Israel,
and served as its fourth prime minister. Born in Kiev, Ukraine,
she emigrated to Wisconsin in 1906. Her political activity
began as a leader in the Milwaukee Labor Zionist Party.

After emigrating to Palestine in 1921, she held key posts in the
Jewish Agency and in the World Zionist Organization. After
Israel proclaimed its independence in 1948, she served as
minister of labor, and then foreign minister. Meir was
appointed prime minister in 1969.

During her administration, she worked for a peace settlement
in the Middle East using diplomatic means. Her efforts at
forging peace were halted by the outbreak of the fourth Arab-
Israeli war. She resigned her post in 1974, but remained an
important political figure throughout her retirement.

Golda Meir's true strength and spirit were emphasized when
after her death in 1978, it was revealed that she had suffered
from leukemia for twelve years.

GOLDA MEIR
1898 - 1978

"*A leader who doesn't hesitate before he sends his nation into battle is not fit to be a leader.*"

＊ ＊ ＊

"*Those who do not know how to weep with their whole heart don't know how to laugh either.*"

＊ ＊ ＊

"*You cannot shake hands with a clenched fist.*"

＊ ＊ ＊

"*I can honestly say that I was never affected by the question of the success of an undertaking. If I felt it was the right thing to do, I was for it regardless of the possible outcome.*"

GOLDA MEIR
1898 - 1978

"*Our school education ignores, in a thousand ways, the rules of healthy development.*"

Elizabeth Blackwell
1820 - 1910
First American Woman Physician

"*You should always know when you're shifting gears in life. You should leave your era; it should never leave you.*"

Leontyne Price
1927
American Opera Singer and
recipient of eighteen Grammy Awards

"*You can't invent events. They just happen. But you have to be prepared to deal with them when they happen.*"

Constance Baker Motley
1921
First Black Woman to become a
Federal Judge in the United States

"*As long as you keep a person down, some part of you has to be down there to hold him down, so it means you cannot soar as you otherwise might.*"

Marian Anderson
1902
First Black Woman to sing solo
at the Metropolitan Opera

"*A child is the root of the heart.*"

Carolina Maria de Jesus
Brazilian Writer

"*Only a marriage with partners strong enough to risk divorce is strong enough to avoid it.*"

Carolyn Heilbrun
American Educator and Writer

"*To be somebody, a woman does not have to be more like a man, but has to be more of a woman.*"

Sally E. Shaywitz
1942
American Pediatrician and Writer

"*People change and forget to tell each other.*"

Lillian Hellman
1907 - 1984
American Playwright and Writer

"I can stand what I know. It's what I don't know that frightens me."

Frances Newton
Historian

"If you want a place in the sun, you've got to put up with a few blisters."

Abigail Van Buren
1918
American Newspaper Columnist and Lecturer

"There is so much that must be done in a civilized barbarism like war."

Amelia Earhart
1898 - 1937?
First Female Aviator

"In order that she may be able to give her hand with dignity, she must be able to stand alone."

Margaret Fuller
1810 - 1850
First American Woman to become
a Foreign Correspondent

"When I say we've had an ideal marriage, I'm not just talking about physical attraction, which I can imagine can wear pretty thin if it's all a couple has built on. We've had that and a whole lot more."

Betty Ford
1918
Former First Lady of the United States
and Civic Leader

"Familiarity, truly cultivated, can breed love."

Joyce Brothers
1925
American Psychologist and Journalist

"No country can advance unless its women advance."

Maie Casey
1891 - 1983
Australian Humanitarian

"We're all in this alone."

Lily Tomlin
1936
American Comedienne and Actress

"Do your job brilliantly and the cream will rise to the top."

Irene Rosenfeld
American Business Woman
Executive Vice President of Kraft — General Foods

"I never really address myself to any image anybody has of me. That's like fighting with ghosts."

Sally Field
1946
American Actress

"We have learned that power is a positive force if it is used for positive purposes."

Elizabeth Dole
1936
United States Labor Secretary

"All love shifts and changes. I don't know if you can be wholeheartedly in love all the time."

Julie Andrews
1935
English Actress and Singer

"My voice has been raised not only in song, but to make the big world outside through me, understand something of the spirit of my beloved country."

Dame Nellie Melba
1861 - 1931
Australian Opera Singer

"Love and respect are the most important aspects of parenting, and of all relationships."

Jodie Foster
1962
American Actress

"If you really want to reach for the brass ring, just remember that there are sacrifaces that go along."

Cathleen Black
American Business Woman –
Publisher of USA Today

"I tried always to do better: saw always a little further. I tried to stretch myself."

Audrey Hepburn
1929
English Actress

"Don't insult a woman with lies, when you can wow her with the truth."

Valerie Salembier
American Publisher of Family Circle
magazine and Senior Vice President of
New York Times Co. Women's magazines

"You have to be willing to step out of the pack and take risks, even jump completely out of your element if that's what it takes."

Carol Bartz
1948
American Business Woman
Chairman and CEO of Autodesk

"I like who I am now. Other people may not. I'm comfortable. I feel freer now. I don't want growing older to matter to me."

Meryl Streep
1949
American Actress

"Power is the ability to get things done."

Rosabeth Moss Kanter
American Business Woman
First Woman Editor of the Harvard Business Review,
Co-director of a consulting firm and
Author of ten books

"I think the key is for women not to set any limits."

Martina Navratilova
1956
Professional Tennis Player

"All marriages require adjustments. There are so many changes to be made all at once."

Grace Kelly
1929 - 1982
American Actress who married
the Prince of Monaco

"I believe that a worthwhile life is defined by a kind of spiritual journey and a sense of obligation."

Hillary Clinton
American Lawyer and Wife of
Govenor Bill Clinton

"You learn more from ten days of agony than from ten years of content."

Sally Jessy Raphaël
American Talk Show Host

"Service is what life is all about."

Marian Wright Edelman
American Founder and President
of the Children's Defense Fund and the First Black Woman
admitted to the Mississippi Bar

"Follow your instincts. That's where
true wisdom manifests itself."

Oprah Winfrey
1954
American Actress and Talk Show Host

"Choose to have a career early and a
family late or choose, like I did, to have a
family early and a career late.
Plan a long life."

Janet Davison Rowley
American Physician who broke ground in the
field of Cancer Genetics

"The success of women in television and
in other fields is because of the whole
women's movement and the changes in
this country."

Barbara Walters
1931
American Journalist, Writer,
Television Producer and Commentator

Great Women Index

Other Books From Celebrating Excellence

Great Quotes from Great Leaders

The Best of Success

Never Never Quit

Commitment to Excellence

Management Magic

Motivational Quotes

Customer Care

Opportunity Selling

Commitment to Quality

America: It's People, It's Pride and It's Progress

Zig Ziglar's Favorite Quotations

Think: Creativity and Innovation

Winning With Teamwork

The Power of Goals

Your Attitude Determines Your Altitude

Motivation Lombardi Style